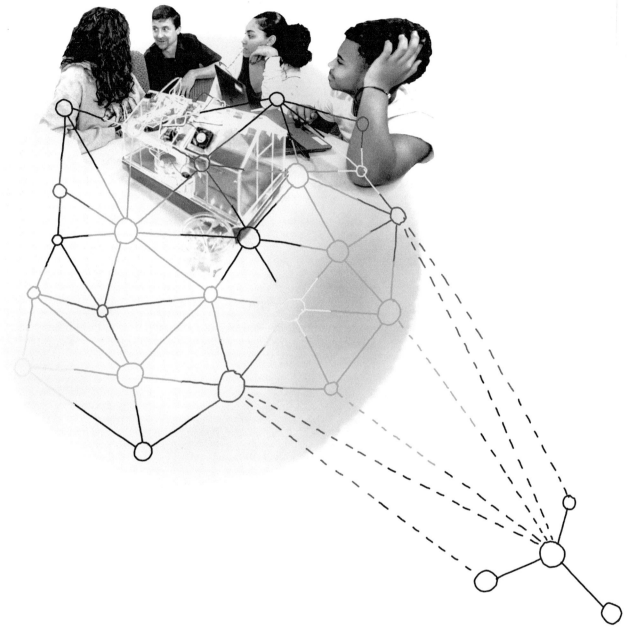

THE CASE FOR ARTS INTEGRATION
THE ALLIANCE FOR THE ARTS IN RESEARCH UNIVERSITIES

ALLIANCE FOR THE ARTS
IN RESEARCH UNIVERSITIES

Published in the United States of America by
Michigan Publishing
Manufactured in the State of Michigan, United States of America on
70# White Offset Smooth, FSC Certified Paper Stock

DOI: https://doi.org/10.3998/mpub.11599226

ISBN 978-1-60785-598-9 (paper)
ISBN 978-1-60785-599-6 (open-access)

THE ALLIANCE FOR THE ARTS IN RESEARCH UNIVERSITIES

The Alliance for the Arts in Research Universities (A2RU) fosters and champions the role of the arts and design in research universities. A2RU supports faculty, students, and academic leadership who seek to better integrate the arts and design into the interdisciplinary, collaborative fabric of their universities, and is committed to supporting the growing body of high-quality scholarly and creative production most attainable when disciplines are free to experiment within and across their boundaries.

MAKING THE CASE FOR ARTS INTEGRATION

Like all A2RU's programs, *The Case for Arts Integration* is grounded in research and developed through integration and synthesis. This resource supports the work of arts integration on-campus, and draws on insights gathered from over 600 interviews with academic leaders, institutional officers, faculty, staff, and students at over 60 research universities. The A2RU research team systematically reviews these insights for evidence of the positive impacts, successful patterns, best practices, recurring challenges, and salient stories of arts integration. Then, working in collaboration with individual faculty, staff, and leadership from across A2RU's partner universities, we translate these insights into practicable amplification tools like this book.

CONNECTING ACROSS CAMPUS

The Case for Arts Integration is a tool for connecting across campus, outlining the "what," "why," and "how" of arts integration. While this book shows how arts integration can function on campus, and its range of impacts, the case it makes is broad and all-encompassing. Each university will want to define what arts integration looks like for them and how it fits into their unique cultural landscape. To support the journey, A2RU offers a companion workbook, a hands-on tool designed to help you map how the arts and arts integration advances your university's mission. As you move through the workbook, *The Case for Arts Integration* becomes a reference, a source for examples and inspiration.

A2RU PARTNERS

Boston University	Texas Tech University	University of Iowa
Carnegie Mellon University	Tufts University	University of Kansas
Dartmouth College	The University of Alabama	University of Maryland
James Madison University	The University of Alabama at Birmingham	University of Michigan
Johns Hopkins University	University of Arizona	University of Nebraska-Lincoln
Kent State University	University of Arkansas	University of Nevada, Las Vegas
Louisiana State University	University of California, Berkeley	University of North Texas
Massachusetts Institute of Technology	University of Cincinnati	University of Texas at Dallas
Michigan State University	University of Colorado Boulder	University of Utah
Northeastern University	University of Colorado Denver	University of Virginia
Oregon State University	University of Florida	University of Wisconsin-Madison
Penn State	University of Georgia	Virginia Commonwealth University
Princeton University	University of Houston	Virginia Tech
Rochester Institute of Technology	University of Illinois at Urbana-Champaign	

WHAT

IS ARTS INTEGRATION?

WHAT IS ARTS INTEGRATION?

Integration can mean different things to different people, and arts integration is no exception. Practitioners take both formal and informal approaches—from thinking in terms of interdisciplinary and transdisciplinary archetypes to simply showing up and working together. Successful integration involves two complementary activities:

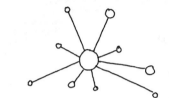

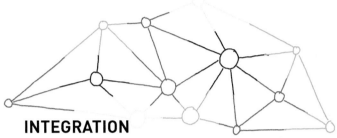

DIFFERENTIATION
Recognizing the distinctions between fields, perspectives, practices, and possibilities.

INTEGRATION
Recognizing the meaningful applications and connections between fields, perspectives, practices, and possibilities—as well as their contingencies.

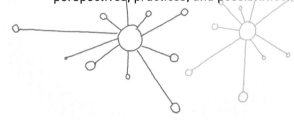

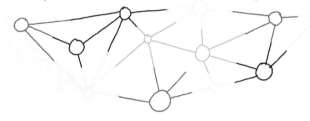

WHAT DO WE MEAN BY "THE ARTS"?

The mindsets and practices of creativity and making – strongly associated with the humanities and the fine, performing, and applied arts & design — rather than the discipline labels themselves.

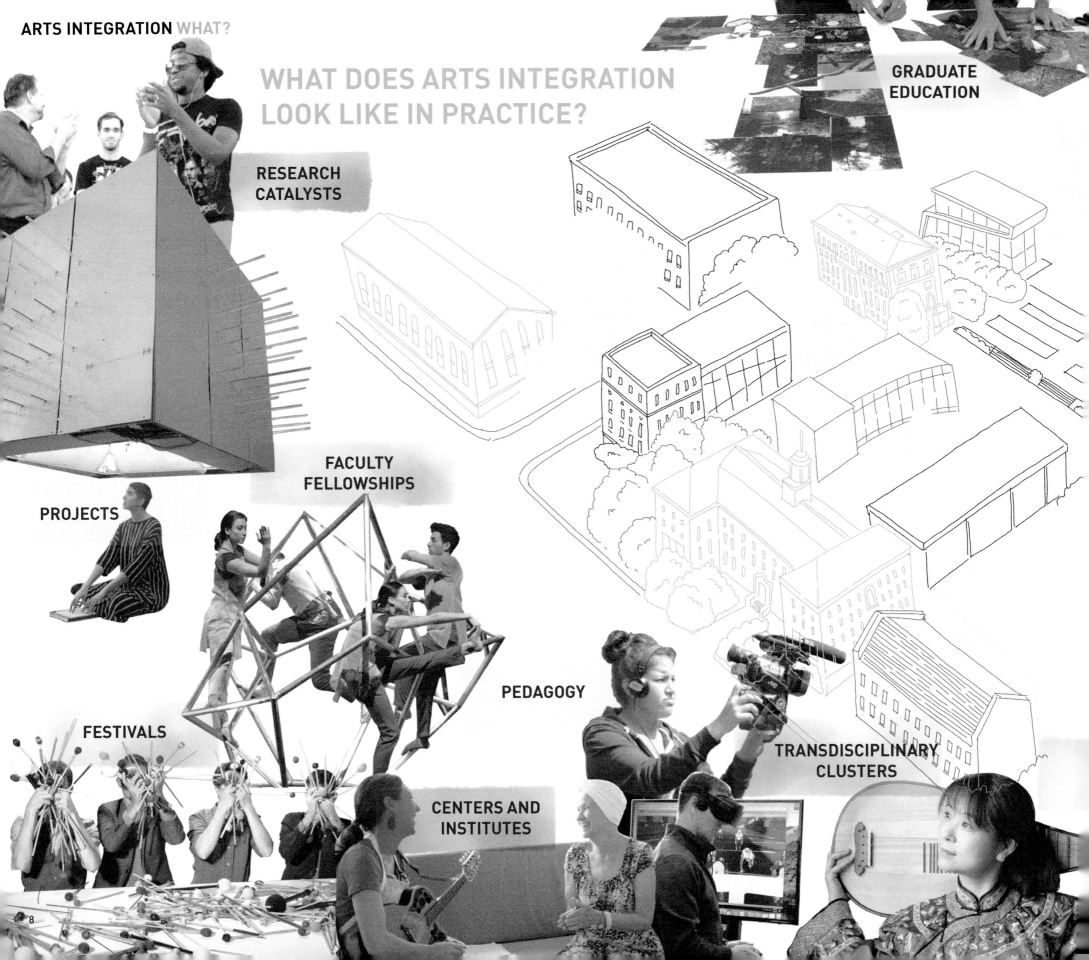

ARTS INTEGRATION WHAT?

WHAT DOES ARTS INTEGRATION
LOOK LIKE IN PRACTICE?

GRADUATE
EDUCATION

RESEARCH
CATALYSTS

FACULTY
FELLOWSHIPS

PROJECTS

PEDAGOGY

TRANSDISCIPLINARY
CLUSTERS

FESTIVALS

CENTERS AND
INSTITUTES

8

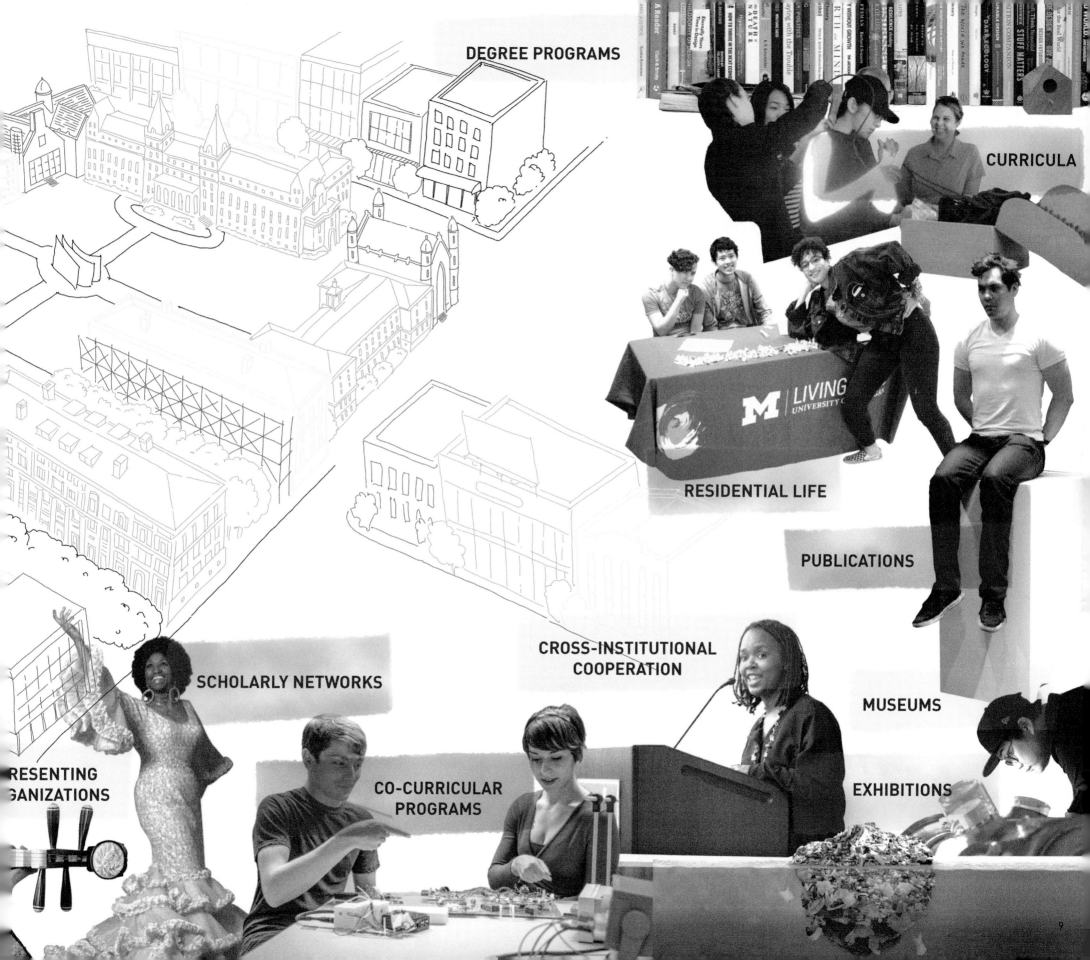

DEGREE PROGRAMS

CURRICULA

RESIDENTIAL LIFE

PUBLICATIONS

CROSS-INSTITUTIONAL COOPERATION

MUSEUMS

SCHOLARLY NETWORKS

RESENTING GANIZATIONS

CO-CURRICULAR PROGRAMS

EXHIBITIONS

9

Centers and Institutes

ARTS RESEARCH INSTITUTE *VIRGINIA COMMONWEALTH UNIVERSITY*

The Arts Research Institute (ARI) at Virginia Commonwealth University frames artistic practice as research, encouraging intellectual inquiry in and through the creative fields. ARI supports faculty with research development, offering a range of technical services including project design, partnership development, dissemination and promotion, and research consultation. It also fosters interdisciplinary collaboration, exploring new directions in creative practice, and the unique contributions of art and design to new knowledge in other fields. Finally, ARI facilitates public dialogue in salons, forums, and galleries, exploring the evolving role of artists and designers in society.

CENTER FOR THE ARTS IN MEDICINE *UNIVERSITY OF FLORIDA*

Through ongoing interdisciplinary research, training programs, and dynamic academic programs, the University of Florida Center for the Arts in Medicine advances arts in medicine, locally and globally. Established in 1996, the Center continues to provide a framework for interdisciplinary collaboration among University of Florida faculty and students, healthcare providers, clinical artists, and our local and global communities. The Center serves as a national model for arts in health, with programming that includes Creating Healthy Communities--a national initiative at the intersection of arts and public health—and graduate and undergraduate programming that situates visual arts, music, theatre, and dance in medicine.

DESIGN INNOVATION INITIATIVE *KENT STATE*

Co-Curricular Programs

The Kent State University Design Innovation Initiative connects a network of existing makerspaces and resource laboratories across the entire university, making them more visible, accessible, and effective in supporting cross-disciplinary collaboration. This network of "Design Innovation Nodes" connects to the "Design Innovation Hub," which serves as an open-access, co-making, idea-generating center. Coursework, co-curricular projects, competitions, hackathons, and grand challenges help to foster kinetic collisions among students, faculty, community, and leading experts from diverse disciplines, addressing complex problems through design. Students and graduates become Design Innovation Fellows, people whose embedded instinct is to create teams of individuals that come from the widest array of backgrounds to tackle the truly big problems facing our world.

ARTSENGINE MOLDWIN PRIZE *UNIVERSITY OF MICHIGAN*

The ArtsEngine Moldwin Prize is designed for an undergraduate students currently enrolled in the Penny W. Stamps School of Art & Design, the Taubman School of Architecture and Urban Planning or the School of Music, Theatre and Dance at the University of Michigan who are interested in exchange and collaboration with students engaged in research practice in an engineering lab. No previous science or engineering experience is required, although curiosity and a willingness to explore are essential. Students receiving the residency spend 20 hours over 8 weeks participating with the undergraduate research team in the lab of Professor Mark Moldwin which is currently doing work in the areas of space weather (how the Sun influences the space environment of Earth and society) and magnetic sensor development. Successful applicants receive $1,000 in support of their time, materials and creative work. Applicants should plan to articulate both their expected contributions to the lab environment as well as the knowledge and skills they hope to gain.

PROGRAM FOR RESEARCH IN THE HUMANITIES *UNIVERSITY OF ILLINOIS*

Cross-Institutional Cooperation

The Illinois Program for Research in the Humanities (IPRH) at the University of Illinois at Urbana-Champaign coordinates and hosts lectures, symposia, and panel discussions on a wide variety of topics, and provides awards that recognize excellence in humanities research to faculty and students. IPRH supports faculty-driven initiatives, and grants fellowships to Illinois faculty and graduate students. IPRH is also the locus for the Mellon-funded Humanities Without Walls consortium, which links the humanities centers at 15 research universities throughout the Midwest and beyond. Leveraging the strengths of multiple distinctive campuses, Humanities Without Walls includes (1) summer workshops for pre-doctoral students in the humanities who want to explore diverse careers in which they can use their expertise and credentials and (2) funding for cross-institutional teams of faculty and graduate students pursuing research that focuses on a grand intellectual challenge.

INTEGRATIVE STUDIES GENERAL EDUCATION REQUIREMENT *PENN STATE*

Curricula

The 6-credit Integrative Studies requirement at Penn State is intended to make integration an explicit part of the General Education program. Integrative Studies courses aim to advance students' ability to comprehend ideas from multiple perspectives, to see connections, and to employ different modes of thinking; one domain is not fully equal to the task of understanding the world around us. Linked Courses provide sustained focus on a single Knowledge Domain, with connections to another course in a different Knowledge Domain, while Inter-Domain courses provide the immediacy of incorporating two Knowledge Domains in the same course. Inter-domain courses include Show Me Where it Hurts: Healthcare and Creative Inquiry, and Meteorology and Visual Arts: To Know is to See.

QUEST *UNIVERSITY OF FLORIDA*

The University of Florida is implementing a revised undergraduate core curriculum called Quest. Quest invites students to grapple with intellectual, social, and real-life questions that extend beyond any one discipline and are suggestive of the kinds of challenges they will face in a complex and interconnected world. The first year offers courses centered in the arts and humanities that explore challenging questions about the human condition, such as *How do people decide what makes life worth living? What makes a society a fair one?* The second year focuses on identities, the third on justice and power, and the senior year on war and peace. Within the first year curriculum, the Center for Arts in Medicine will offer a course entitled The Arts and Compassion. The course explores compassion – or how people respond to human suffering with empathetic action – through the visual, literary and performing arts.

CDASH *UT DALLAS*

Curriculum Development in the Arts, Sciences, and Humanities (CDASH) is both a resource for faculty interested in art-science-humanities curriculum and a data collection point where curriculum can be surveyed for innovation and sustainability. A project by the ARTSCILAB at University of Texas at Dallas, the site hosts a broad range of curricula, sourced from instructors around the country, that combine the performing and visual arts (music, dance, theatre, film, visual arts and new media) and the sciences. Users contribute syllabi and other resources for their own courses, and search the database for curricula that interest them. In-person classroom, online, and hybrid blended courses are all represented.

PHD IN TRANSITION DESIGN *CARNEGIE MELLON UNIVERSITY*

Degree Programs

The PhD in Transition Design at Carnegie Mellon University seeks to develop future design leaders with the capacity to envision and realize transitions to sustainable futures. Students develop their own research interests within the broad framework of transition design, and the four-year program cultivates the knowledge, skills, and literacies to design systems-level change, over long horizons of time. Complex problems must be addressed through ecologies of interventions that draw on multiple design specializations, alongside expertise from other disciplines. This sees service designers, social designers, communication designers and product designers, working alongside ecologists, anthropologists, philosophers, economists and political scientists.

SCIENCE GALLERY - DETROIT *MICHIGAN STATE UNIVERSITY*

Exhibitions

Acting as a bridge between the city of Detroit and the Michigan State University campus in East Lansing, Science Gallery Detroit features experiences aimed at 15- to 25-year-olds that blend art, science, and technology in connective, participative, and surprising ways. Science Gallery Detroit is a lightweight 'pop-up,' and part of the Global Science Gallery Network, a highly collaborative peer group of Science Gallery nodes located in leading cultural and technological hubs worldwide. Each Science Gallery generates exhibitions and programs with the local creative and scientific community. These can be shared through the global network and beyond, increasing public understanding and access to high quality science-art, at a significantly reduced program cost for each individual gallery.

COLLABORATIVE ARTS RESEARCH INITIATIVE (CARI) *UNIVERSITY OF ALABAMA*

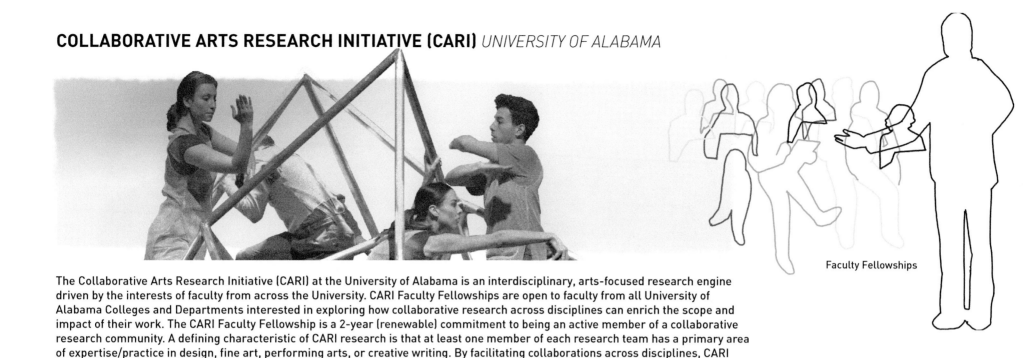

Faculty Fellowships

The Collaborative Arts Research Initiative (CARI) at the University of Alabama is an interdisciplinary, arts-focused research engine driven by the interests of faculty from across the University. CARI Faculty Fellowships are open to faculty from all University of Alabama Colleges and Departments interested in exploring how collaborative research across disciplines can enrich the scope and impact of their work. The CARI Faculty Fellowship is a 2-year (renewable) commitment to being an active member of a collaborative research community. A defining characteristic of CARI research is that at least one member of each research team has a primary area of expertise/practice in design, fine art, performing arts, or creative writing. By facilitating collaborations across disciplines, CARI maximizes the impact of faculty arts research, while enriching the University, local, and regional communities.

ACCELERATE: ACC SMITHSONIAN CREATIVITY AND INNOVATION FESTIVAL *VIRGINIA TECH*

Festivals

Virginia Tech and the Smithsonian Institution present ACCelerate: ACC Smithsonian Creativity and Innovation Festival. The festival celebrates creative exploration and research happening at the nexus of science, engineering, arts and design (SEAD), and features interactive installations from across the fifteen Atlantic Coast Conference (ACC) schools. In addition, seven scholars from across the ACC participate in the Bridging Chasms initiative, a series of "exchanges" between the scholars. During an exchange, each participant attempts to explain some essential elements of their discipline to their partner, an equally accomplished individual with different disciplinary expertise. The initiative seeks to identify what enables and what impedes understanding across disciplines.

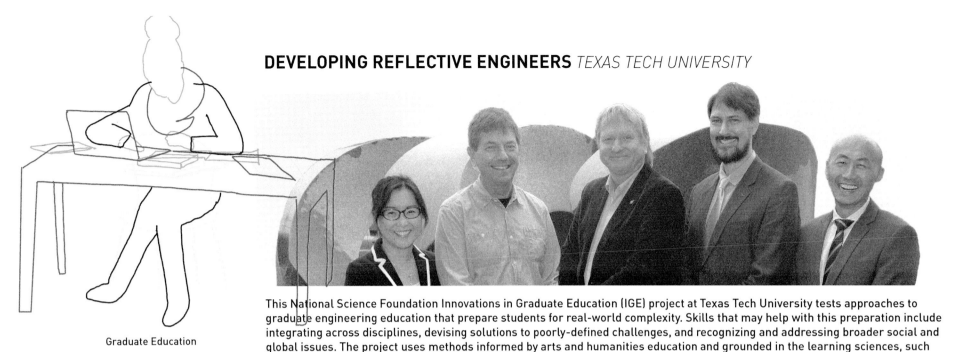

Graduate Education

DEVELOPING REFLECTIVE ENGINEERS *TEXAS TECH UNIVERSITY*

This National Science Foundation Innovations in Graduate Education (IGE) project at Texas Tech University tests approaches to graduate engineering education that prepare students for real-world complexity. Skills that may help with this preparation include integrating across disciplines, devising solutions to poorly-defined challenges, and recognizing and addressing broader social and global issues. The project uses methods informed by arts and humanities education and grounded in the learning sciences, such as visual thinking strategies to develop observational skills, computer-simulated ethical/moral dilemmas to prepare for real world complexity, and team projects to practice reflective engineering. The purpose of these techniques is to enhance reflective reasoning and connect that reasoning to engineering.

INNOVATIONS IN GRADUATE EDUCATION *UNIVERSITY OF GEORGIA*

With its National Science Foundation Innovations of Graduate Education (IGE) award, the University of Georgia seeks to fundamentally enhance how STEM students are educated by engaging them in creativity-based training methods from the arts. The project recruits a cohort of students in the early stages of graduate study, from STEM disciplines and from arts disciplines, to address issues in the local watershed. With facilitation by faculty members from STEM and arts disciplines, students gain practical experience sharing disciplinary viewpoints and developing collaborative frameworks for complex problem solving. The initiative will assess students' abilities to shift thinking, generate novel ideas, and effectively collaborate with one another. Successful elements will be incorporated into a scalable training model that will be available to other institutions.

INTEGRATED ARTS RESEARCH INITIATIVE *UNIVERSITY OF KANSAS*

Museums

The Integrated Arts Research Initiative (IARI) at the Spencer Museum of Art at the University of Kansas (KU) rethinks the academic art museum as an active participant in research across the sciences and humanities. This initiative expands the Spencer's Arts Research Collaboration initiative (2011–2015), which developed pathways for collaboration between the Museum and faculty, staff, and students across the University. IARI proposes to transform the art museum into an active hub for collaborative research between the arts and other disciplines through research fellowships, visiting scholars and creative specialists, forums, and publications. Semester- and year-long research fellowships through IARI allow KU students and faculty to engage in deeper collaborations with the Museum.

MOON ARK *CARNEGIE MELLON UNIVERSITY*

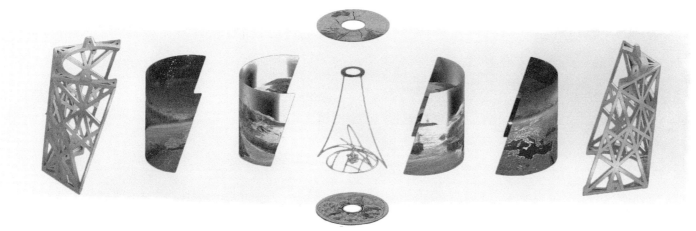

In 2020, Carnegie Mellon University is sending the first museum to the Moon aboard an Astrobotic lander. The project, called The MoonArk, is a highly collaborative sculpture that poetically integrates the arts, humanities, sciences, and technologies. Weighing a combined total of six ounces, it contains hundreds of images, poems, music, nano-objects, mechanisms, and earthly samples intertwined through complex narratives. The MoonArk is designed and engineered to last thousands of years, projecting humanity in a beautiful and significant way. Fabrication of the MoonArk has instigated innovation in material science, technology, and the arts, engaging 250 contributors from across disciplines.

Pedagogy

INDIGENOUS MAKING AND SHARING *UNIVERSITY OF WISCONSIN*

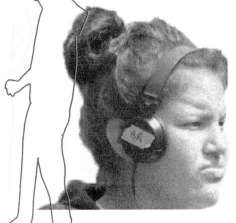

Indigenous Arts and Sciences (IAS) is a University of Wisconisin collaboration with Native Nations throughout the state. Through work with youth, families, communities, and teachers, IAS addresses the need for culturally relevant learning experiences in the context of environmental education. IAS emphasizes community, place, and culture in approaches to ecological restoration, and brings together people interested in linking environmental and health concerns to academic achievement in science, math, social studies, language, and the arts. In addition to professional development for teachers, IAS involves year-round youth programs that support family-school-community connections. Through a series of Summer Institutes, Earth Partnership IAS professional development programs engage educators, community members, college students, scientists, natural resource specialists, and K-16 teachers in ecological restoration and water stewardship rooted in Indigenous knowledge.

NEURO-EDUCATION INITIATIVE AND ARTS INTEGRATION PARTNERSHIP *JOHNS HOPKINS*

The Johns Hopkins Neuro-Education Initiative is part of a School of Education arts-integration partnership with Margaret Brent Elementary/Middle school. The partnership includes professional development for teachers, staff support, enhanced curriculum, upgraded technology, programming both inside and outside of the classroom, and a wide array of curriculum-related collaborations. Arts integration specialists work onsite with educators at Margaret Brent to teach the neuroscience behind arts integration, share lesson plans, and foster the Brain Targeted Teaching model developed by JHU Vice Dean of Academic Affairs Mariale Hardiman. Hardiman's research shows that incorporating the arts into science lessons can help low-achieving students retain more knowledge, and that using arts-integrated instruction to teach science increases students' long-term retention of scientific content as effectively as, or better than, conventional science instruction.

COURSE DEVELOPMENT GRANTS *UNIVERSITY OF MICHIGAN*

Presenting Organizations

The University Musical Society (UMS) Course Development Grants incentivize faculty at the University of Michigan to integrate performance into their courses; proposed courses are either new or substantially revised to meaningfully incorporate one or more UMS performances into the class. The grants include $1,000 in salary supplement and $500 in course development funds, as well as curricular and practical support. Grantees in recent years have come from the humanities as well as Dentistry, Biophysics, Mechanical Engineering, Social Work, Nursing, and a diverse array of other disciplines. Grantees gather to brainstorm and exchange ideas about performance in their courses, and UMS staff meets individually with grantees, helping to match course content and goals with season performances.

IN TERMS OF PERFORMANCE *UC BERKELEY*

Publications

In Terms of Performance is a keywords anthology designed to provoke discovery and generate shared literacies across disciplines. It features essays and interviews from more than 50 prominent artists, curators, presenters, and scholars who reflect on common yet contested terms in contemporary cultural practice. The publication is produced by The Pew Center for Arts & Heritage, Philadelphia and the Arts Research Center. It is co-edited by Shannon Jackson, director of the Arts Research Center, and Paula Marincola, executive director of the Pew Center.

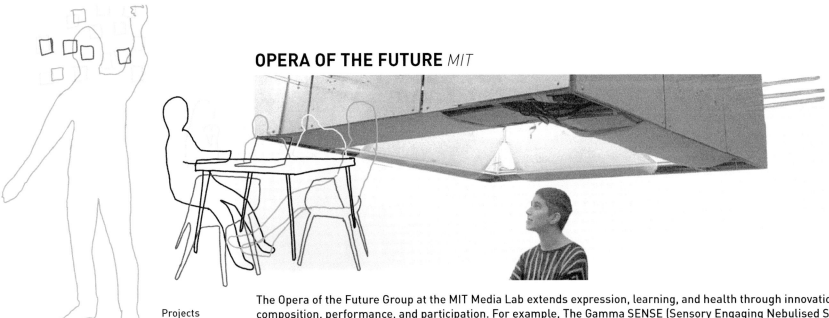

Projects

OPERA OF THE FUTURE *MIT*

The Opera of the Future Group at the MIT Media Lab extends expression, learning, and health through innovations in musical composition, performance, and participation. For example, The Gamma SENSE (Sensory Engaging Nebulised Scent Experience) device project is a medical/musical instrument that delivers multisensory gamma stimulation through auditory, visual, and olfactory channels. The Gamma SENSE device aids in the testing and identification of the olfactory perceptive triggers which recruit and sustain identified cognitive frequencies. The device is part of a larger exploration of 40 Hz frequencies and Alzheimer's prevention/reduction.

CATALYST GRANTS *KENT STATE*

Research Catalysts

The Kent State University College of the Arts awards Catalyst Grants to faculty for interdisciplinary research and creative projects involving undergraduate students. Applicants are encouraged to design their projects by innovating across disciplines and engaging students as meaningful collaborators. Catalyst grants are available for up to $5,000. Faculty must collaborate with at least one faculty/staff from another school in the College of the Arts, from another college at Kent State University, or a partner external to KSU. All projects must also include the involvement of undergraduate students as research collaborators.

ENTREPRENEURIAL FACULTY SCHOLARS + FIND A RESEARCHER *UNIVERSITY OF UTAH*

The Entrepreneurial Faculty Scholars program at the University of Utah nurtures a community of creative innovators and entrepreneurs. It serves both as matchmaker for cross-disciplinary collaborations and as a collegial support network for those seeking to translate academic discoveries and creations into the world. The program supports innovative faculty who create companies, provide artistic experiences to expanding communities, and find practical applications for ideas and concepts. Meanwhile, the Find a Researcher database contains listings of University of Utah faculty and graduate students who are research topic experts and potential research collaborators. Users can search for people by entering names, research keywords, departments, international experience keywords, and equipment.

RED HOT RESEARCH *UNIVERSITY OF KANSAS*

The Commons at the University of Kansas presents the Red Hot Research series as a forum for research exchange. These 6-minute, slide-based lightning talks introduce audiences to an idea, and KU Researchers to the work of their colleagues. The sessions address questions within current research using the perspectives of many disciplines, and they develop interest and expertise in collaborative research teams.

Residential Life

LIVING ARTS *UNIVERSITY OF MICHIGAN*

The Living Arts interdisciplinary residential community on the University of Michigan's North Campus brings together 115 undergraduates in the arts, architecture, engineering, and other fields to explore innovation, creativity, and collaboration. Living Arts provides an open, playful environment that encourages students to generate and pursue new ideas. The program offers weekly classes and monthly workshops by distinguished faculty and working professionals from the fields of engineering, architecture, visual arts, film, music performance and composition, dance, and theater. All Living Arts students take an interdisciplinary class together and work on collaborative projects. They also receive support for the creation of their own programming and events, and mentorship from older Living Arts students.

TRECS *VIRGINIA TECH*

Transdisciplinary Clusters

The nine transdisciplinary research and education communities (TRECS) at Virginia Tech identify methods for different disciplines to develop curricular, research, and external engagement in ways that inform one another and thus strengthen transdisciplinary connections. The Creativity and Innovation area melds the exploration of innovative technologies and the design of creative experiences with best practices for developing impact-driven and meaningful outcomes and solutions. Creativity & Innovation draws students, faculty, and external partners from a broad range of disciplines including Architecture, Arts, Business, Communication, Computer Science, Creative Writing, Design, Education, Engineering, History, and Chemistry.

4S 'MAKING AND DOING' SESSIONS *SOCIETY FOR SOCIAL STUDIES OF SCIENCE*

Scholarly Networks

The Science Technology and Society (STS) Making and Doing Program is an Annual Meeting session for Society for Social Studies of Science (4S) members to share scholarly practices of participation, engagement, and intervention in their fields of study. Making and Doing highlights scholarly practices for producing and expressing STS knowledge and expertise that extend beyond the academic paper or book. By increasing the extent to which 4S members learn from one another about practices they have developed and enacted, the initiative seeks to improve the effectiveness and influence of STS scholarship beyond the field and/or to expand the modes of STS knowledge production.

HASTAC *DARTMOUTH UNIVERSITY, GRADUATE CENTER AT THE CITY UNIVERSITY OF NEW YORK (CUNY)*

HASTAC (Humanities, Arts, Science, and Technology Alliance and Collaboratory) is an interdisciplinary community of humanists, artists, social scientists, scientists, and technologists. HASTAC's 16,000+ members from over 400+ affiliate organizations share ideas, news, tools, research, insights, pedagogy, methods, and projects--including Digital Humanities and other born-digital scholarship--and collaborate on various HASTAC initiatives. HASTAC is governed by a dynamic, interdisciplinary Steering Committee, and its leadership and administration is shared between hubs located at the Graduate Center at the City University of New York (CUNY) and Dartmouth College. Each year, hundreds of scholars from the HASTAC community come together in one space for a conference, hosted by affiliate organizations at locations around the globe.

WHY

ARTS INTEGRATION MATTERS

SUPPORTS UNIVERSITY GOALS

Arts integration improves research, promotes student success, and engages and serves the public.
Below are the six most common university mission statements and how arts integration supports them.

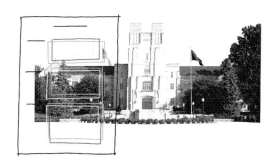

EMPOWERING STUDENTS WITH TRANSFORMATIVE EDUCATIONAL EXPERIENCES THAT PREPARE THEM FOR SUCCESS

Arts-integrated classrooms afford students conceptual and hands-on experiences that prepare them to succeed in a range of endeavors post-graduation, and create fulfilling lives.

SUPPORTING FACULTY DEVELOPMENT WITH ACADEMIC COMMUNITY AND A ROBUST EXCHANGE OF IDEAS

Promoting collaboration between the arts/design and other parts of campus enables faculty--as co-teachers and as research partners--to engage with concepts, practices, and people that can refresh and inspire.

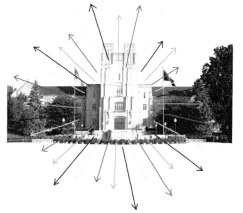

DISCOVERING, PRESERVING, CRITICALLY EXAMINING, TRANSMITTING, AND ADVANCING KNOWLEDGE

Integrating the arts with, for example, STEM fields engenders excellence in teaching, research, scholarship, and creative endeavors--avenues that intersect and ultimately lead to knowledge diversity.

MODELING A DIVERSE, WELCOMING, INCLUSIVE, AND DEMOCRATIC SOCIETY

Inherent in arts integration initiatives is a coming together of diverse ways of knowing and working; their success depends on the mutual respect among interdisciplinary players. Such initiatives become microcosms of the university.

PROMOTING THE CULTURAL, ECONOMIC, AND INTELLECTUAL CONDITION OF THOSE BEYOND THE CAMPUS WALLS

Whether a university focuses this aspect of its mission on its alumni, state, nation, or the world, the arts can play a key role in this outward-facing, service-oriented goal. From publicly-engaged artworks to arts-integrated research that results in life-changing medical discovery or engineering innovation, the impacts of arts integration in the university resonate well beyond the campus.

SETTING THE STANDARD AS A NATIONAL AND INTERNATIONAL LEADER

Successfully implementing arts integration programming positions universities to lead, anticipating--rather than merely reacting to--future challenges.

ANTICIPATES EDUCATIONAL AND SOCIETAL TRENDS

FROM

TRADITIONAL DEGREE TIMELINES

IVORY TOWER

TRADITION

STANDING COMMITTEES

POLARIZED WORKPLACE SKILLS

ARTS & CULTURE

CHANGING STUDENT DEMOGRAPHICS

TO

PERSONALIZED LEARNING PATHWAYS
Driven by new education access points and greater demand for flexibility, individualization, and customized learning experiences, multigenerational learners are pushing for Personalized Learning Pathways that move beyond traditional degrees and into formats that better match their own interests, career options, and emerging needs. (Educause 2019; IFTF, AI Forces Shaping Work & Learning in 2030; NASEM Branches Report 2018)

PUBLICLY ENGAGED KNOWLEDGES
As options for DIY knowledge expand through and beyond universities, scholarly research and creative practices become more open, collaborative, and real-time. Public engagement emerges as a core pillar of research universities: to maintain relevance, demystify big science, broaden the strategic impacts of the university's mission, and bridge increasingly elite forms of knowledge production with competing viewpoints for living, working, and interacting in the world. (Future Knowledge Ecosystems, IFTF, 2010; UM Conceptualizing Public Engagement, 2019)

DISRUPTION & MIGRATION
Major weather, health, and regional community disruptions, prompted by the planet's warmer atmosphere, will be felt in different ways by different regions and university constituencies. Universities increasingly serve as a focal point for preparedness and prevention for their diverse communities, networks of students, staff, faculty, research agendas, and funding portfolios (USGCRP/NCA4).

POP-UP COMMUNITIES
As research universities become more loosely connected, distributed, and shape-shifting organizations, it is important for academic leadership, teaching teams, and research groups to have the ability to quickly scan the landscape of opportunities, knowledge, social networks, and potential challenges. Pop-up Panels become the organizational currency for getting things done efficiently, side-stepping outdated institutional norms. (IFTF: Beyond Organizations, 2018; Educause 2019)

RECIPES FOR SUCCESS
The distribution of workforce skills and careers is becoming more polarized than ever, but advanced analytical tools for recognizing and adapting to emerging workforce and labor market trends are providing key insights to those students, employers, and educators with the best access. As a result, equipped students can tailor their unique strengths, personalities, and experiences to assemble diverse combinations of skills that create the most meaningful work and career outcomes for them. (Alabdulkareem et al, 2018; Anderson, 2017).

AUTHENTICITY & AGENCY
Driven by issues of class, identity, market ideologies, and winner-take-all allocations of resources, the arts trend towards three primary cultural attractors: big, fun, lavish entertainment spectacles for mass appeal; bespoke material and social aesthetics as private status symbols for the elite upper echelons of society; and culture-making as a politically dissident activity for making identities that challenge prevailing norms. (from: Ben Davis, 2018, Three Tendencies of Future Art, e-flux journal #89)

INTERSECTIONAL INSTRUCTIONAL DESIGN
The shifting demographics of student bodies has always been a trend in higher education. However, there is a new recomposition underway that redefines demographic profiles altogether in order to reshape instructional practices, the ontological assumptions of educators, and access to knowledges resources and learning experiences.

IMPACTS AND BENEFITS

A lively and engaged arts presence across the university benefits various groups uniquely.

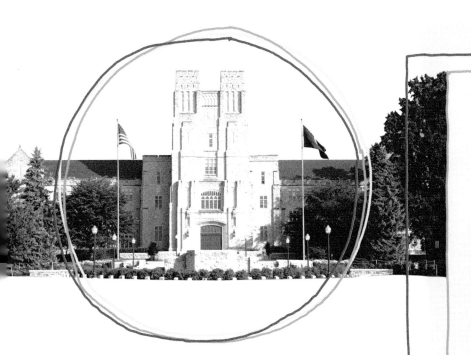

STUDENTS

- exposure to new perspectives
- improves mental health, including improved social bonds, campus spirit, reduced stress, and a sense of belonging
- expands worldviews from working with others whose backgrounds differ from their own
- increases critical thinking, content mastery, creative problem solving, teamwork, and communication skills
- a richer experience of themselves and their peers
- preparation for jobs and further academic pursuits after graduation

UNIVERSITIES

- opens pathways to funding streams, public engagement, and broader impacts
- attracts different undergraduate populations, affecting enrollment as universities face demographic shifts
- offers a broader, deeper, more meaningful curriculum
- equips graduates with the collaborative, critical thinking, and communications skills that the 21st century demands
- attracts exceptional faculty talent
- enhances staff satisfaction through vibrant campus life

FACULTY

- develops new research methodologies and partnerships
- improves the quality of research
- broadens the societal impact of research
- enhances or transforms disciplines through interdisciplinary influence
- builds connections across and beyond the academy
- enriches teaching through cross-disciplinary collaboration
- engages an array of different learners
- promotes complexity in the learning experience

EMPLOYERS/INDUSTRY

- tenacity and self-efficacy
- avenues for growth mindsets
- cross-sector know-how
- creative intelligence
- community affiliation
- connection to cultural traditions
- adept at managing uncertainty
- socio-cognitive and sensory-physical skills

REGIONAL COMMUNITY

- contributes to a region's economic development
- creates vibrant community identity, quality of life, civic engagement, and pride
- provides opportunities to build social capital
- vibrant arts scene on campus leads to a greater understanding of the university's connection and value (e.g., presence of theater or gallery)
- allows community members to engage with the arts more fully

HOW
MIGHT WE APPROACH ARTS INTEGRATION?

COMMON STEPS IN THE JOURNEY

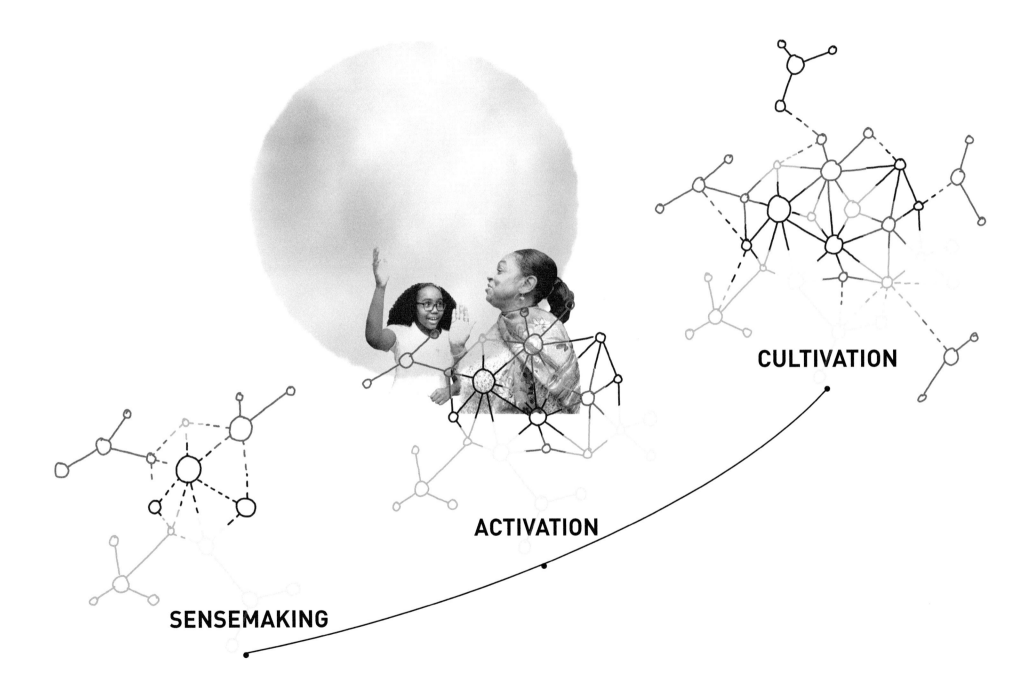

CULTIVATION

ACTIVATION

SENSEMAKING

SENSEMAKING

These institutions are looking for ideas and examples from peers and advocacy to reinforce early energy.

KEY NEEDS

- drawing inspiration
- looking at examples and case-making
- finding frameworks, definitions, and clarification
- learning from context and history
- asset mapping and diagnosing institutional strengths and obstacles

ACTIVATION

Having established several ongoing initiatives, these institutions are less focused on basic advocacy for arts integration, and more concerned with operational, policy, and practice issues.

KEY NEEDS

- matching with peers for advice and hands-on help
- operational and policy guidance
- internal visioning, alignment, and coordination
- time, space, resources
- research insights and deep experience

CULTIVATION

Artistic process and practice are deeply and durably integrated across institutional efforts, not only in teaching, research, and service, but also in institutional planning, strategy, incentive systems, and infrastructure. Current academic and institutional leadership promote these ideals, and they also seek out these values in any search for new leadership.

KEY NEEDS

- strategy, incentive systems, infrastructure, leadership, partnerships, evaluation, foresight, sharing
- peer-to-peer expertise and review
- benchmarking, evaluation, and reporting

BEST PRACTICES

WITNESS EACH OTHER'S PRACTICE

Take the time to visit unfamiliar "home turf." See what colleagues from different fields do when they are at work.

CONTEXT

Physically going to an unfamiliar space, such as a studio or lab, and watching and listening to what goes on there is an efficient way to learn about the practices and cultures of other domains. Seeing a colleague at work *in situ* can help build a shared body of knowledge and mutual respect.

"...the sharing of process is really significant to me. Because someone can take a look at the outcome, the product, and go, 'Wow that product is beautiful, I have no idea how you got there. It seems like you just got there by fancying around in your studio until the muse struck you on your head and then off you went.' No, there's an actual practice to that, that can be taught and learned, and honed, and perfected. Bringing those two things together can be useful, if you just share that much. How do you do your work and how do I do mine?"

Faculty Artist
A2RU campus interview

"In the last three years that we've had the collaborative category, the students that have done the best jobs are the ones where the arts student has gone to the science student's laboratory, and spent an afternoon or two just seeing what goes on, and learning some of the lingo, and just getting an idea of what's happening. Then the science student has gone to the arts student's studio and has watched them do their creative thing. Those seem to be the pairs of students that make the most progress on getting an idea together."

Instructor
A2RU campus interview

"One way we also dealt with each other's disciplines was we just would meet regularly. I would often go out for meetings with her whole group of students and just listen to all her projects and I learned a lot. I actually did some, studied a little basic programming to try to learn some languages that I was encountering in their area. And we did, once we had a workshop, we invited the engineers down to come and engage with some dance practices. So those were ways in which we try to maybe just open the door to see the complexity of each other's disciplines."

Faculty Collaborator
A2RU campus interview

A CROSS-CUTTING THEME

Use a single concept or theme--like water, or the concept of induction, or the color yellow--to provide a common touchpoint. Faculty and students engage with it according to their disciplines; they also meet with those from other disciplines to share their ideas and imagine ways they might work together.

CONTEXT

Many universities are structured to support a lone researcher and domain-specific expertise. When universities provide cross-cutting themes as reference points, they encourage interdisciplinary collaboration, knowledge networking, and mutual understanding. They create a forum for people from disparate fields--sculpture and medicine, for example--to meet on common ground.

"Theme Semesters provide intellectual and cultural immersion in a particular topic across U-M. Students combine coursework with lectures, museum exhibits, music or theater performances, film series, and more. This exploration doesn't just stay inside the academy, either. Theme Semester events are generally open to the public and are done frequently in collaboration with community organizations."

Theme Semester
College of Literature, Science, and the Arts at the University of Michigan

"The spring 2019 Theme Semester, "American Dream," asks how can our university equitably serve in the 21st century. What do Americans desire? How can we imagine an American dream that embodies the values and aspirations of all Americans? How do we ensure that all Americans have an equitable say, that all exert agency over their lives, that we treat everyone with compassion and respect? How do we imagine a dream that replaces exclusion with inclusion? What does the American Dream mean to the most diverse generation in this country's history?"

Spring 2019 Theme Semester
The University of Iowa

BEST PRACTICES

ESTABLISH SHARED SPACES

By establishing physical spaces specifically designated--or even designed--for faculty and students from different fields to interact, universities promote interdisciplinarity by design. These spaces should be flexible enough to accommodate different practices.

CONTEXT

In many universities, interdisciplinarity exists in a liminal zone between schools and departments; as a result, there often is no physical space where arts integrated work can happen. Designated shared spaces are the ready-made home for interdisciplinary, team-taught courses (which often are difficult to schedule into traditional spaces) and provide a venue for interdisciplinary research teams to meet. In addition, if an interdisciplinary space remains open and available to students, it becomes an incubator for creative collaboration.

The establishment of a dedicated physical space acknowledges that encountering difference in the material reality of another human has different implications from the disembodied world of on-screen interaction.

The Commons at the University of Kansas is intended as a catalyst for unconventional thinking, interdisciplinary inquiry, and unexpected discoveries across the sciences, arts and humanities. A partnership between the Biodiversity Institute, the Hall Center for the Humanities, and the Spencer Museum of Art, The Commons is both a physical and intellectual space where people come together to establish common ground from which they may express and explore uncommon ideas for the common good. This vibrant and active space serves many purposes, including Coffee @ The Commons, a venue for conversation between interested members of the community and a visiting expert, and Red Hot Research, a series designed specifically for research exchange which features short, slide-based talks that introduce audiences to an idea.

https://thecommons.ku.edu/

The heart of the Lassonde Studios student residence at the University of Utah is the "garage" on the first floor. A mostly open space with moveable furniture, it features co-working space, private offices for startups companies, cafe, lounge space, and a prototyping area with 3D printers, sewing machines, hand tools, laser cutter and more. Any student at the University of Utah is welcome to use the "garage." "We want to accelerate the time it takes for students to see their ideas become a reality, and we want to give them a place where they can meet and form interdisciplinary teams," said Taylor Randall, Dean of the David Eccles School of Business.

https://lassonde.utah.edu/university-of-utah-breaks-ground-on-lassonde-studios-building/

ESTABLISH ARTS PERSONNEL IN DEDICATED LEADERSHIP POSITIONS

Arts integration champions in leadership positions craft policy and structures that institutionalize arts integration. They minimize red tape, build bridges across disciplines on campus, and create a supportive environment for these initiatives. Furthermore, arts-specific high-level administrative positions make the university's commitment to arts integration evident to peer institutions and the public.

CONTEXT

Designated arts leaders are in positions to align policies and practices with institutional interdisciplinary values. Without that top-down support, collaborators must fight upstream to accomplish their work and have it properly credited in a system that is not designed to accommodate it. The presence of a Vice-Chancellor or Vice-President for the Arts also signals to the public and to peer institutions that the arts are a valued part of the university's strategic plan.

"What we were lacking, until [the new Dean] came, which is the critical role I think organizationally for this, was someone who was truly faculty, who was not only committed to these ideas but in the position to begin to make it happen."

Faculty Member
A2RU campus interview

In January 2019, the University of Arizona announced the appointment of Andrew Schultz to the newly created position of Vice President for the Arts. Robert Robbins, President of the University of Arizona, commented, "Going through strategic planning, I kept emphasizing that student success and research were important, but I thought we were missing the arts...This position shows the university sees the arts on par with other programs." Schultz is charged with integrating the arts into non-arts curricula and elevating the profile of UA arts not only on the campus, but nationally and even internationally.

https://tucson.com/entertainment/ua-creates-new-position-to-boost-the-arts-on-campus/article_583bfda6-f8c3-5c83-a05e-704c990a82fb.html

Shannon Jackson serves in the faculty leadership position of Associate Vice Chancellor for the Arts and Design at UC-Berkeley. In his 2015 announcement of her appointment, Berkeley Chancellor Nicholas Dirks noted that Jackson's role promotes "...the advancement of the arts as a constitutive element of undergraduate education, as a distinctive feature of our research and creative profile, and as a key part of our public mission given how arts and design can help form a vibrant bridge between our campus and our local and international community."

http://arts.berkeley.edu/announcement-regarding-faculty-leader-of-arts-and-design/

BEST PRACTICES

INCENTIVIZE INTERDISCIPLINARY ACTIVITY THROUGH POLICY

University leaders create policy that aligns incentives for faculty and students with arts-based and interdisciplinary values. For example, for faculty, statements in Tenure and Promotion policy detail how arts or interdisciplinary activity "counts" toward faculty members' professional trajectory. For students, robust University-wide arts or interdisciplinary requirements provide academic incentives.

CONTEXT

There may be institutionalized dis-incentives for arts participation and interdisciplinarity--for faculty who find a disconnect between their interdisciplinary work and Tenure and Promotion requirements (for example), and for students who would like to expand the boundaries of their disciplinary learning but are restricted by curricular requirements. Establishing concrete rewards makes participation in arts and arts-integrative activities a natural choice.

"And so something that I come up against very, very often is for example, you can't get tenure. You don't get points, you don't get credit if you do collaborative work. Nobody knows where to put it. Tenure in my field anyway is entirely dependent on writing a book; it's not dependent on creating programs or doing any sort of practice-based research as I've been talking about a lot with my other colleagues. So there's that. Just basic tenure and promotion standards."

Faculty Member

"There is an undergraduate certificate program that draws students from business, engineering, and arts. But a lot of the curricula in the School of the Arts are structured so tightly that they prevent them [the students] from stepping outside their disciplines and taking these courses. They've had a good population of students that have participated, but it could have been more. We are finding that even with our entrepreneurship courses that we are offering, that the curricula are so tightly packed that the students don't have much flexibility.

Director, Center for Entrepreneurship
A2RU campus interview

MAKE THE IMPLICIT, EXPLICIT

When collaborators ask questions and explain their own work explicitly, they surface unstated norms and expectations. With set-aside time, preferred ways of working together, tacit assumptions about roles and responsibilities, and implicit biases emerge. If left unspoken, any of these can become an obstacle to success.

CONTEXT

When collaborators from across campus arrive at the table--be they upper-level leadership forging a new policy, or members of a research or creative team-- they bring the expectations and languages of their particular disciplinary cultures. Trouble arises when these are left implicit, when collaborators assume that their expectations and languages are shared and understood around the table. The resulting misunderstandings can bring an interdisciplinary collaboration to a halt or, at the institutional level, can result in exclusion when those who don't know the implicit mechanisms behind policy (for example, what "counts" for tenure and promotion) struggle to succeed. Memoranda of Understanding and team charters can help make the terms explicit; even the process of working on one together is a beneficial exercise.

"Well, I bring lots of research [to the table]. I bring articles. So, for instance, my colleagues in the College of Ed didn't understand what arts integration was. They said, 'We're going to create a center and use art to teach math and use art to teach reading,' and I said, 'That's fine, but here are some articles on what art integration is.'"

Faculty Member
A2RU campus interview

A2RU has produced a set of Implicit/Explicit cards for those charged with tenure and promotion policy. Each card bears a question relating to issues of tenure and promotion. Play reveals which elements of an institution's RTP practices are explicitly addressed in policy and which remain tacit, helping players recognize the cultural biases present in institutional norms, processes, and policies. Additionally, players use the color-coded cards to identify the roles and processes that are most relevant to them. This can serve as a first indication of which areas may need more clarification, and provide a jumping-off point for critical discussion. The cards are also useful in mentor meetings, in groups who compare and share key insights and themes, and in conversations along the way in any individual or institutional RPT journey.

HOW DO YOU MEASURE SUCCESS?

Individual universities have unique reasons for integrating the arts on campus, and unique goals for their programming. "Success" is defined for each institution based on those goals. By assessing or evaluating arts integrative programming, institutions can check whether goals are being met, improve programming, and advocate for its value.

Administrators or outside evaluators can assess any program's success by considering whether benchmarks for the goals have been met. Consider the following common institutional goals, and sample benchmarks for their success:

IMPROVES RESEARCH

QUANTITATIVE MARKERS

- projects supported and/or funded
- prizes and awards
- publication, exhibition, and performance metrics
- intellectual property and patents
- invitations to participate
- venues and channels where work is featured
- number of new areas of inquiry

QUALITATIVE MARKERS

- nature of the research product
- peer and audience feedback
- prestige/reputation of publication or venue
- press and stories
- appropriation of project elements or material
- grantor feedback
- flourishing of project, project line of inquiry, and collaborations

PROMOTES STUDENT SUCCESS

QUANTITATIVE MARKERS

- test scores
- outside formal review results
- number of alumni employed
- number of alumni continuing academic trajectory
- number of prizes and awards
- tenacity, persistence, and sustained engagement
- spatial reasoning
- communication skills
- leadership skills
- problem-solving
- organization and time management
- wellbeing

QUALITATIVE MARKERS

- instructor evaluation of exam, assignment, or student-produced artifact using grades or rubrics
- student reflection
- alumni happiness, health, economic security
- press
- type of alumni employment
- type of institution for continuing academics
- patience
- self-efficacy and self-confidence
- abstract thinking
- critical thinking
- envisioning and imaging
- empathy
- tolerance for ambiguity and/or risk
- reflection, contemplation
- responsibility
- work ethic, discipline
- respect
- observation, attention to detail
- technical arts skill
- fulfillment

HOW DO YOU MEASURE SUCCESS?

ENGAGES AND SERVES THE PUBLIC

QUANTITATIVE MARKERS

- attendance numbers at event
- number of participants
- measures of outcomes
- tenacity, persistence, and sustained engagement

QUALITATIVE MARKERS

- recognition of risks and barriers
- openness to growth
- communications skill
- motivations to engage
- needs & goals articulated
- norms & expectations
- positive responses (surveys, interviews)
- earned media and press
- improved community image and status

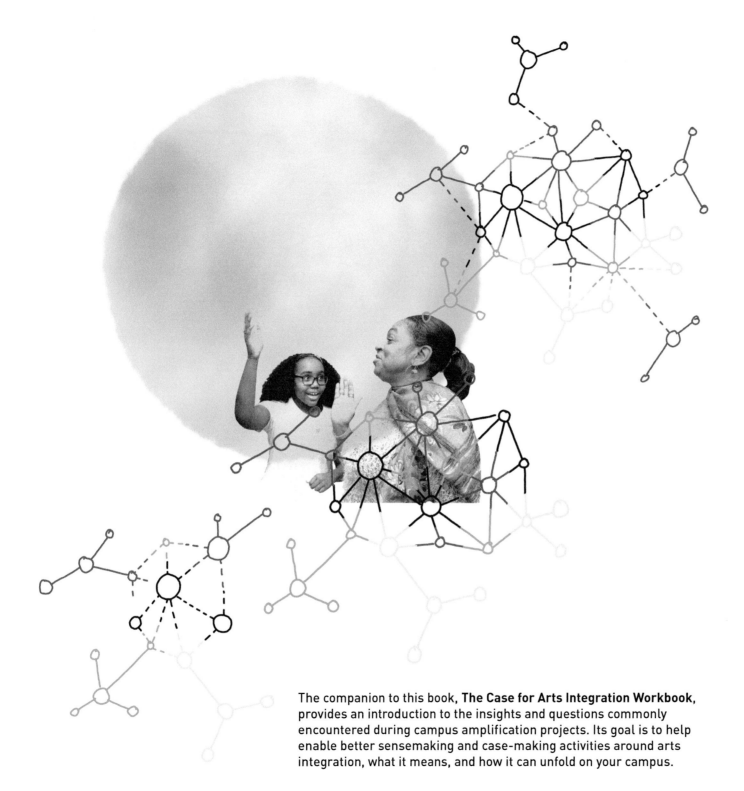

The companion to this book, **The Case for Arts Integration Workbook,** provides an introduction to the insights and questions commonly encountered during campus amplification projects. Its goal is to help enable better sensemaking and case-making activities around arts integration, what it means, and how it can unfold on your campus.

"IF ART DOESN'T MAKE US BETTER, THEN WHAT ON EARTH IS IT FOR?"

– Alice Walker

Arts Integration is happening. This book and the companion workbook are tools to help you be at the forefront of an exciting movement and transformation that is taking place in universities everywhere.

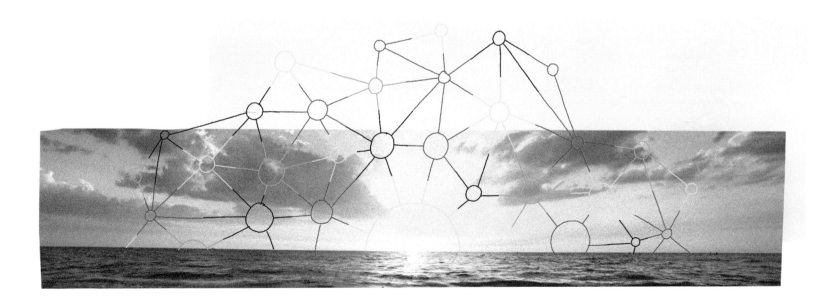

CREDITS

The Sensemaking-Activation-Cultivation framework draws from A2RU's research, work by Andrew Taylor on behalf of A2RU, and XPLANE's Activation Curve framework (https://www.xplane.com/activationcurve). The framework has roots in diffusion theory and the concept of organizational sensemaking, including:

Gioia, D. A., & Chittipeddi, K. (1991). Sensemaking and sensegiving in strategic change initiation. Strategic management journal, 12(6), 433-448.

Tarde, G. (1903). The laws of imitiation, (E. C. Parsons, Trans.). New York: Holt.

Rogers, E.M. (2003). Diffusion of Innovations (5th ed.). New York: Free Press.

Ryan, B., & Gross, N. C. (1943). The diffusion of hybrid seed corn in two Iowa communities. Rural Sociology, 8(1), 15.

Weick, K. E. (1984). Small wins: Redefining the scale of social problems. American Psychologist, 39(1), 40.

Weick, K. E. (1995). Sensemaking in organizations (Vol. 3). Sage.

Some context-making activities in the Common Case Workbook are adapted from concepts in:

Lee, V.S., Hyman, M.R., & Luginbuhl, G. (2007). The concept of readiness in the academic department: A case study of undergraduate education reform. Innovative Higher Education, 32: 3-18

The Common Case definition of integration draws from work on Integrative Complexity in cognition, decision making, and social psychology:

Suedfeld, P., & Rank, A. D. (1976). Revolutionary leaders: Long-term success as a function of changes in conceptual complexity. Journal of Personality and Social Psychology, 34, 169-178.

Suedfeld, P., Tetlock, P.E., & Streufert, S. (1992). Conceptual/integrative complexity. In C. P. Smith (Ed.), Motivation and personality: Handbook of thematic content analysis (pp. 393-400). Cambridge, UK: Cambridge University Press.

Feist, G. J. (1994). Personality and working style predictors of integrative complexity: A study of scientists' thinking about research and teaching. Journal of Personality and Social Psychology, 67(3), 474.

Suedfeld, P., & Tetlock, P. E. (2001). Individual differences in information processing. Blackwell handbook of social psychology: Intra-individual processes, (pp. 284-304).

Conway III, L. G., Suedfeld, P., & Tetlock, P. E. (2018). Integrative complexity in politics. In The Oxford Handbook of Behavioral Political Science. Oxford, UK: Oxford University Press.

Complementary definitions for integration may also be found in:

Barber, J. P. (2012). Integration of learning: A grounded theory analysis of college students' learning. American Educational Research Journal, 49(3), 590-617. (Education)

Barry, A., Born, G., and G. Weszkalnys (2008) Logics of Interdisciplinarity. Economy and Society, 37(1): 20-49. [Anthropology]

Burt, R. S. (2004). Structural holes and good ideas. American Journal of Sociology, 110(2), 349-399. (Sociology)

Ludwig, D. (2016). Overlapping ontologies and Indigenous knowledge. From integration to ontological self-determination. Studies in History and Philosophy of Science Part A, 59, 36-45. (Anthropology and Philosophy)

Mansilla, V. B., Duraisingh, E. D., Wolfe, C. R., & Haynes, C. (2009). Targeted assessment rubric: An empirically grounded rubric for interdisciplinary writing. The Journal of Higher Education, 80(3), 334-353. (Interdisciplinary Studies)

Julia Marshall (2010) Five Ways to Integrate: Using Strategies from Contemporary Art, Art Education, 63:3, 13-19. (Art Education)

O'Rourke, M., Crowley, S., & Gonnerman, C. (2016). On the nature of cross-disciplinary integration: A philosophical framework. Studies in History and Philosophy of Science Part C: Studies in History and Philosophy of Biological and Biomedical Sciences, 56, 62–70. (Philosophy of Science)

Pohl, C., van Kerkhoff, L., Hirsch Hadorn, G., and Bammer, G. (2008). Integration in G. Hirsch Hadorn et al. (eds.), Handbook of Transdisciplinary Research. Springer. (Interdisciplinary Studies)

Repko, A. (2007). Integrating interdisciplinarity: How the theories of common ground and cognitive interdisciplinarity are informing the debate on interdisciplinary integration. Issues in Interdisciplinary Studies. 25, 1-31. (Interdisciplinary Studies)

Rhoten, D., & Pfirman, S. (2007). Women in interdisciplinary science: Exploring preferences and consequences. Research Policy, 36(1), 56-75. (Interdisciplinary Studies)

References for Trends in Higher Education and Society:

Alabdulkareem, A., Frank, M. R., Sun, L., AlShebli, B., Hidalgo, C., & Rahwan, I. (2018). Unpacking the polarization of workplace skills. Science Advances, 4(7), eaao6030.

Alexander, B., Ashford-Rowe, K., Barajas-Murph, N., Dobbin, G., Knott, J., McCormack, M., Pomerantz, J., Seilhamer, R., & Weber, N. (2019). EDUCAUSE Horizon Report 2019 Higher Education Edition (pp. 3-41). EDU19.

Anderson, K. A. (2017). Skill networks and measures of complex human capital. Proceedings of the National Academy of Sciences, 114(48), 12720-12724.

Aurbach, E.L, Kuhn, E., & Niemer, R.K. (2019). Working Draft 3.0 of the Michigan Public Engagement Framework. URL: https://docs.google.com/presentation/d/1J5YP-fqht9Psg3auNYDDI4I04jSp0_nR8YGZOPSWLnw/edit#slide=id.g4f97d01030_2_85

Davis, B. (2018). Three Tendencies of Future Art. e-flux journal #89. URL: https://www.e-flux.com/journal/89/179149/three-tendencies-of-future-art/

Institute for the Future. (2018). AI Forces Shaping Work & Learning in 2030. Palo Alto: IFTF. URL: http://www.iftf.org/fileadmin/user_upload/images/ourwork/Work___Learn/IFTF_Lumina_AI_Forces_Work_Learn.pdf

Institute for the Future. (2018). Beyond Organizations: New Models for Getting Things Done [map]. Palo Alto: IFTF. URL: http://www.iftf.org/fileadmin/user_upload/downloads/ourwork/InstitutefortheFuture_GoogleCloud_Beyond_Organizations_map_Reader_031319_01.pdf

National Academies of Sciences, Engineering, and Medicine. (2018). The integration of the humanities and arts with sciences, engineering, and medicine in higher education: Branches from the same tree. National Academies Press.

Townsend, A., Soojung-Kim Pang, A., & Weddle, R. (2010). Future Knowledge Ecosystems: The Next Twenty Years of Technology-Led Economic Development. Palo Alto: Institute for the Future. URL: http://www.iftf.org/uploads/media/SR-1236%20Future%20Knowledge%20Ecosystems.pdf

Reidmiller, D. R., Avery, C. W., Easterling, D. R., Kunkel, K. E., Lewis, K. L. M., Maycock, T. K., & Stewart, B. C. (2018). Fourth National Climate Assessment, Volume II: Impacts, Risks, and Adaptation in the United States. Washington, DC, USA: US Global Change Research Program.

COLLABORATIVE ARTS RESEARCH INITIATIVE Image by Norah Zuniga Shaw
https://cari.ua.edu/wp-content/uploads/2019/01/Obj21_3DAlignmentAnim.jpeg

ACCELERATE: ACC SMITHSONIAN CREATIVITY AND INNOVATION FESTIVAL Photo by Virginia Tech
https://i1.wp.com/acceleratefestival.com/wp-content/uploads/2019/04/DSC_3989.jpg?zoom=2&fit=1200%2C1200

DEVELOPING REFLECTIVE ENGINEERS Photo by Phil Marshall
https://today.ttu.edu/posts/2018/10/Images/Taraban_et_al_grant_rs.jpg

INNOVATIONS IN GRADUATE EDUCATION Photo courtesy of Mark Callahan

INTEGRATED ARTS RESEARCH INITIATIVE Photo by IRI
https://spencerart.ku.edu/sites/default/files/jaeyoung-park.jpg

MOON ARK Image by Moon Ark http://moonarts.org/moon-museum/#earth

INDIGENOUS MAKING AND SHARING Photo by Indigenous Arts and Sciences (IAS)
https://earthpartnership.wiscweb.wisc.edu/wp-content/uploads/sites/155/2018/02/DSC01738-900x600.jpg

NEURO-EDUCATION INITIATIVE AND ARTS INTEGRATION PARTNERSHIP Photo by Will Kirk / Homewood Photography
https://api.hub.jhu.edu/factory/sites/default/files/styles/landscape/public/phoenix_0.jpg?itok=KunVfKI6

COURSE DEVELOPMENT GRANTS UNIVERSITY OF MICHIGAN Photo: Wu Man of China NCPA Orchestra by Stephen Kahn

IN TERMS OF PERFORMANCE Image by Jérôme Bel, Le dernier spectacle (The last performance), 1998. Photo by Herman Sorgeloos.

OPERA OF THE FUTURE Photo by Pricilla Capistrano
https://dam-prod.media.mit.edu/thumb/2018/05/04/IMG-1934.JPG.1400x1400.jpg

CATALYST GRANTS KENT STATE
https://www.kent.edu/sites/default/files/styles/larger/public/page/Fall%20for%20the%20Arts%202.JPG?itok=M6GJYbOq

ENTREPRENEURIAL FACULTY SCHOLARS + FIND A RESEARCHER Photo by University of Utah
https://efs.utah.edu/images/retreat.jpg

RED HOT RESEARCH Photo by The Commons at the University of Kansas
https://thecommons.ku.edu/sites/thecommons.ku.edu/files/RedHotResearchBanner.jpg

LIVING ARTS Photo by ArtsEngine
https://livingarts.engin.umich.edu/wp-content/uploads/sites/320/2017/08/DSC_0004-768x512.jpg

TRECS VIRGINIA TECH https://vtnews.vt.edu/content/vtnews_vt_edu/en/articles/2019/04/icat-creativityandinnovationday/jcr:content/article-image.transform/xl-medium/image.jpg

4S 'MAKING AND DOING' SESSIONS Photo by SOCIETY FOR SOCIAL STUDIES OF SCIENCE
https://www.4sonline.org/images/md18-hdr.jpg

HASTAC Image Credit: Fania Records
https://www.hastac.org/sites/default/files/styles/post_image/public/upload/images/post/celia-cruz-i-introducing-i-album-art.jpg

CREDITS

Research and Authors: Gabriel Harp, Veronica Stanich, Stephanie Gioia
Design/Illustration: Rich Moore, Stephanie Gioia

This project was made possible by the Alliance for the Arts in Research Universities (A2RU), Future Work Design, and ArtsEngine at the University of Michigan with support from the Andrew W. Mellon Foundation.

The authors gratefully acknowledge the support received from the National Endowment for the Arts for research on impacts.

With thanks to Mark Callahan, JR Campbell, Maryrose Flanigan, Elizabeth Gray, Mary Beth Leigh, Deb Mexicotte, Marvin Parnes, Deb Pickman, and Emily Ryan for their valued input during the design process. Special thanks to Maryrose Flanigan and Deb Mexicotte for earlier iterations and prototyping of the amplification guidebook and workshop experience.

We are also grateful for the guidance of those who helped shape the initial direction for this work: Jim Agutter, Laurie Baefsky, Daragh Byrne, Sarah Cunningham, Kevin Hamilton, Ben Knapp, Anthony Kolenic, Bruce Mackh, Deb Mexicotte, Gunalan Nadarajan, Patricia Olynyk, Marvin Parnes, Andrew Schulz, Xin Wei Sha, Tamara Underiner, the A2RU Executive Committee, and many more.

Lastly, we are grateful to A2RU partner universities for their past, current, and ongoing support.